ELSIE STEPHENS

CULTIVATING MENTAL STRENGTH THROUGH SELF-DISCIPLINE

Mastering the Art of Self-Control for
Mental Resilience
(2024 Guide for Beginners)

Copyright © 2023 by Elsie Stephens

All rights reserved. No part of this publication may be reproduced, stored or transmitted in any form or by any means, electronic, mechanical, photocopying, recording, scanning, or otherwise without written permission from the publisher. It is illegal to copy this book, post it to a website, or distribute it by any other means without permission.

First edition

This book was professionally typeset on Reedsy.
Find out more at reedsy.com

Contents

I Part: 1

1	Introduction	3
2	Chapter 1: The Journey of Success: Continuous Progress, Not...	6
3	Chapter 2: Unveiling the Realities of Motivation	11
4	Chapter 3: The Power of Your Choices	14
5	Chapter 4: Discovering the Genuine Purpose of Your Existence	17
6	Chapter 5: Discovering Your True Desires and How to Attain...	20
7	Chapter 6: The Unexpected Reality of Happiness	23
8	Chapter 7: Harnessing the Power of Optimism	27
9	Chapter 8: Embracing Failure for Success	30
10	Chapter 9: Harnessing Zen Philosophy for Goal Achievement	33
11	Chapter 10: Embracing Self-Discipline the Shaolin Way	36

II Part: 2

12	Chapter 11: Cultivating Focus and Self-Discipline through...	43
13	Chapter 12: Embracing Action Over Attempt	46
14	Chapter 13: The Essential Principles of Achievement	48
15	Chapter 14: Embracing the Journey	50
16	Chapter 15: Mastering Patience and Resisting Temptation	52
17	Chapter 16: Harnessing Negative Emotions for Success	55
18	Chapter 17: Sturgeon's Law & The Pareto Principle	58
19	Chapter 18: Morita Therapy	62

20	Chapter 19: Preventing Burnout	65
21	Chapter 20: Embracing Change - Overcoming the Status Quo...	68
22	Chapter 21: The Dunning-Kruger Effect	71

I

Part: 1

1

Introduction

Some individuals appear to effortlessly possess everything - enviable jobs, perfect bodies, and attractive partners. They even muster the energy to hit the gym each morning! Their unyielding self-confidence makes them seem almost divine to the rest of us. Admittedly, I may have exaggerated a bit; no one's life is truly flawless. Yet, some among us come remarkably close. What sets these fortunate few apart from the majority? What is the driving force behind their consistent successes and unending opportunities? You've likely observed that these exceptional individuals share a remarkable trait: they remain optimistic and composed even in the face of chaos.

Consider those enduring extreme conditions - soldiers on near-impossible missions or explorers navigating harsh climates for months. Others, like Buddhist monks in the Zen tradition, devote their days to prayer and meditation, forsaking material temptations for spiritual growth at the highest level. What fuels their determination? What motivates them? The answer lies in a single word: self-discipline. It's not merely luck that propels them forward. While genetics might grant some people a head start in terms of appearance or happiness, what truly elevates an ordinary individual to extraordinary heights is razor-sharp focus, unwavering perseverance, and the ability to persist when others give up. In the pages of this book, you will unravel their secrets.

If you've ever pondered why you can't seem to reach your full potential, this guide is your long-awaited solution. If your dreams have remained stagnant, get ready for a life-changing experience. You're about to uncover the core principle behind every successful athlete, CEO, and performer. You will learn how individuals like Navy SEALs face danger head-on and emerge victorious.

Prepare to be surprised; motivation alone isn't a reliable foundation for true greatness. Even those who love their jobs or have discovered their life's purpose don't always wake up brimming with enthusiasm. In life, it's not the most motivated who triumph; it's the most self-disciplined. As you will soon discover, motivation serves as a delightful side dish, not the main course, in the realm of self-discipline.

Moreover, happiness isn't a prerequisite for success. In fact, the pursuit of happiness often leads us astray. Understanding what truly drives us as human beings - hint: it's not just money - and fulfills our deepest needs enables you to transform your mindset and attain military-level self-discipline.

Why does this topic matter to me? I didn't grasp the significance of self-discipline until my early thirties. Despite excelling in various roles within HR departments of well-known corporations, I felt something was missing. I sensed a lack of control over my own career. Regardless of my position's seniority, my job role and paycheck were always in someone else's hands.

My typical pattern involved applying for an exciting job, acclimating to the company culture for a year, and then feeling a sense of restlessness around the 18-month mark. I'd start daydreaming about quitting my corporate career and becoming self-employed. However, the idea of taking charge of my life seemed daunting. How would I stay motivated? Who would hold me accountable? Anxiety gripped me; I stood at a crossroads.

What changed my trajectory? A single conversation. One morning, a senior colleague, Mark, laughed at my ambition to set up my own business and travel the world as a consultant. His skepticism washed over me, and for a moment, I doubted myself. However, I chose a different path. I delved into positive psychology and self-development, discovering the keys to achieving my dreams.

I had been asking the wrong questions all along. I had mistakenly believed I needed unwavering self-assurance and constant motivation to succeed. Countless hours of reading, reflection, and experimentation later, not only do I run my HR consultancy, but I have also compiled my favorite self-discipline strategies in this book. I want to free others from self-doubt. If you truly desire to enhance your self-discipline and transform your life, you can. I now lead a life beyond my wildest dreams a decade ago, and yes, I consider myself highly self-disciplined. I'm not flawless; I'll share my mistakes as we progress through this book. If I can do it, so can you.

This book comprises two parts. The first equips you with the knowledge to shift your mindset from uncertainty to unwavering self-discipline. You'll explore insights from psychology, philosophy, and even the military, understanding motivation and what drives change.

The second part delves deeper, focusing on practical strategies to supercharge every aspect of your life. You'll learn how routines, goal-setting, and techniques like Morita Therapy will propel you to new heights.

Self-discipline isn't taught in schools, leaving it up to us as adults to reclaim our willpower. Thankfully, we live in an age of information, where psychological theories and techniques are readily accessible. I've become addicted to self-development, and once you read this book, you'll understand why. From psychologists to monks, numerous people have invaluable lessons to teach us about self-discipline. It's my privilege to share this priceless knowledge with you.

2

Chapter 1: The Journey of Success: Continuous Progress, Not Just a Flash of Triumph

If you are genuinely dedicated to achieving success, you must have a realistic understanding of what it truly entails. For most people, the notion of "success" evokes an image of someone reveling in their hard-earned victory. It might bring to mind an athlete receiving a medal on the podium, a CEO finalizing a billion-dollar deal, or someone reaching their desired weight after a challenging diet. What do all these scenarios share? They are all based on the misconception that success is the outcome of working tirelessly toward a single, measurable goal, often judged by external parties. Perhaps this perspective is ingrained in us due to the way our education system functions. Everything is reduced to grades and numerical scores, with the focus placed more on a single letter or digit than the journey taken to achieve it.

In reality, success is not a solitary accomplishment or even a series of triumphs. It's an ongoing process. Successful individuals comprehend that victory is a mindset and actively nurture it every day. Ever heard the adage, "It takes a long time to become an overnight success"? It's a cliché because it's undeniably true. No one wakes up one day miraculously having attained everything they desired without putting in any effort. This isn't how the real world operates. If you tend to indulge in magical or wishful thinking, you need to break free from that habit promptly if you wish to master self-discipline and accomplish anything significant. You aren't exempt from the fundamental rules of the universe. If you desire something, you must learn patience and derive satisfaction from hard (and intelligent!) work.

Moreover, goals, once achieved, often demand continual maintenance. If your definition of "success" only encompasses the moment you reach a goal, you risk neglecting to sustain your results. Consider the common scenario of someone trying to lose weight. Most of us can relate to this experience. How often have you attempted to shed a few pounds, only to regain the weight twice as fast as you lost it? I, for one, have gone through a similar cycle multiple times, albeit in my case, I was striving to increase my muscle mass. I would make promising gains but then lose them after a couple of months, leading to immense frustration. Sustaining the healthy eating and exercise habits that contributed to the initial weight loss requires immense self-discipline. The fact that most dieters regain the weight they've lost is a testament to this reality. If you approach weight loss solely with the final number in mind, you're setting yourself up for long-term failure.

The Japanese have long recognized the importance of viewing success as a process rather than an event. The philosophy of Kaizen, which translates to "improvement" or "good change" in English, advocates building on success through continuous small changes. While predominantly used in business contexts, Kaizen is a valuable tool for anyone interested in self-development. According to the Kaizen Institute UK, the core principles of this philosophy emphasize that "good processes bring good results" and success is likely when you "take action to identify and correct root causes of problems."

Kaizen urges us to critically assess how we are attempting to achieve our goals. Most individuals decide on a desired outcome but give little thought to the methods they will use or how they might adjust their approach along the way.

For instance, you might set a goal to "lose twenty pounds using a high-fat, low-carb diet over a three-month period." But what if, four weeks into your diet, you've lost very little weight and aren't enjoying most of the foods you're eating?

Typically, most dieters would quit, perhaps taking a break before attempting to motivate themselves to try again. However, a Kaizen practitioner would analyze what worked well and consider adjustments to enhance their chances of success. For example, while their exercise routine might be beneficial for their overall well-being, it might not be significantly impacting their weight. Applying Kaizen principles, they could make minor alterations with substantial effects on the final outcome, such as working out more frequently for shorter durations.

Embracing a Kaizen approach also prevents falling into the "when...then" thinking trap. When success is perceived as an event, there's a tendency to forget that laying the foundations is necessary before reaping the rewards. Have you ever heard someone say, "When I get a great job, I'll be happy" repeatedly, yet they never take steps to change their situation? This is the epitome of "when...then" thinking. Kaizen challenges us to see success as a cycle of achievement, improvement, further achievement, more improvement, and so on. It assumes that our potential is never completely fulfilled; there is no end point. Things can always be better, and we need to proactively identify the path that efficiently leads us there.

In my case, I aspired to establish my own business. The challenge was that I often got caught up in fantasizing about the day when everything would magically fall into place, forgetting that I would need to take numerous small steps along the way. Every time I reminded myself that I needed to create a business plan, establish a budget, and devise a marketing strategy, my brain would shut down. I would tell myself that I would get around to it "someday," believing that I would be ready to embark on the next phase of my life. For years, that day never arrived. If I hadn't delved into self-discipline, I might

CHAPTER 1: THE JOURNEY OF SUCCESS: CONTINUOUS PROGRESS, NOT...

still be stuck in an office, making a decent living but not truly enjoying my life.

When I finally sat down to outline a business plan, it quickly became apparent that further research was necessary. I spent weeks exploring my target market, evaluating online platforms to reach potential clients, and consulting my contacts for recommendations and word-of-mouth marketing strategies. At that point, having recently acquainted myself with the Kaizen philosophy, I was open to revising my plans multiple times as new information emerged. Although it required significant effort, it was also empowering. I no longer expected to get everything right on my first attempt, reducing my anxiety about venturing out on my own.

Taking the initial step and being prepared for imperfect outcomes is crucial, as it also helps you escape the trap of "when...then" thinking. When you become excessively fixated on a specific outcome, which may or may not materialize in the future (especially if you're waiting around for a burst of motivation, which may never come), you miss out on the opportunity to savor life in the present. Zen practitioners emphasize that all we truly have is this present moment. The past is irretrievable, and there's no way to alter what has already occurred. The future is yet to unfold, and even if we can anticipate it to some extent, unforeseen events might always catch us off guard. While we can cherish memories of the past and aspire for the future, our lives can only be lived in the present.

Therefore, daydreaming and half-heartedly planning what you desire instead of actively transforming your ambitions into reality amounts to squandering valuable time. Once you comprehend the substantial amount of time necessary to achieve and sustain any notable level of success, you'll be less inclined to tolerate this mindset in yourself or others. No one knows how much time they have left on this planet, and idly letting it slip away is a tremendous waste.

So, how can you genuinely start translating your most cherished plans into action? It might seem logical to assume that motivation is the key to sustaining the energy needed to pursue success over an extended period. However, as you'll soon discover in the next chapter, motivation isn't as enchanting as you might think.

3

Chapter 2: Unveiling the Realities of Motivation

How often have you heard someone utter phrases like, "I just can't find the motivation today," or "I'd love to do X, Y, and Z if only I had the motivation"? Perhaps you've caught yourself saying something similar. Most of us have been taught to believe that if we feel motivated to do something, it will eventually get done. We live under the assumption that if we wait long enough to feel motivated or somehow muster the willpower, everything will miraculously become easier. This concept sounds great in theory. Motivation has likely worked for you on occasion. For instance, you might have been motivated to spend hours searching for the perfect gift for your loved ones, striving to make them happy. In this case, motivation could propel you through endless hours at the mall or monotonous evenings comparing prices online.

However, when it comes to substantial tasks such as losing weight, starting a business, or writing a novel, motivation alone doesn't cut it. Sure, you might experience a surge of enthusiasm at the project's outset, but with time, your motivation is bound to fluctuate. This is because once the reality of the situation sets in, and you realize the hard work required to achieve your goal, your motivation inevitably declines. It is at this juncture that you need to tap into other resources to push through, highlighting the importance of self-discipline and cultivating positive habits.

Dr. Kelly McGonigal, a psychologist from Stanford University, specializing in willpower and self-discipline, explains that when faced with a challenging task, two aspects of our personality clash. One part envisions the future and comprehends that enduring hardships and tolerating deprivation will be worthwhile. Another part craves instant gratification, seeking quick results and feeling frustrated when goals aren't met effortlessly. Overcoming setbacks and reaching goals involves tapping into the part of ourselves that sees the bigger picture, enabling us to confront challenges. I delve deeper into this internal conflict and its resolution in my other book, "Emotional Intelligence Training."

This internal struggle was a significant hurdle for me when contemplating leaving my 9-5 job and transitioning into a self-employed consultant. Despite having compelling reasons for this change, facing mundane tasks related to my business, such as creating a marketing plan, left me feeling disheartened. I realized that I didn't need to feel ecstatic about the tedious aspects; I just had to ensure they were completed without being overly critical of myself.

For further insight into why motivation alone isn't sufficient for achieving significant results, let's turn to an unexpected source – the special forces. Consider the Navy SEALs, an elite military unit known for its rigorous training and operations. These officers are required to undertake perilous tasks under various conditions, whether underwater, in the air, or on land. Their training is intense, with only 20% of trainees completing the initial phase. Few individuals would naturally feel motivated to endure such rigorous daily challenges. However, their success isn't solely reliant on motivation.

A crucial element contributing to their achievements is momentum. Naval Admiral William H. McRaven, a former SEAL trainee, shared a valuable lesson he learned during his training. Instructors inspected each trainee's bed meticulously, believing that the act of making the bed triggered a sense of momentum, propelling them forward to tackle other tasks. Similarly, I've found that initiating a task, no matter how small, often generates enough momentum to power through even the most unpleasant chores.

If you've always believed that motivation must precede action, it might be difficult to accept the idea that you can accomplish tasks without fervently wanting to do them. However, the belief that motivation precedes action is limiting because genuine and spontaneous motivation is rare. If you're skeptical, experiment with the momentum concept mentioned above. Just start, and you'll realize that action begets action, potentially leading to motivation as a positive byproduct.

In essence, motivation can be beneficial, especially when dedicated to a cause or set of ideals. Consider the numerous individuals who dedicate their lives to charity work or join religious orders. I'm not suggesting dismissing motivation entirely. Instead, view it as an occasional bonus that can make self-discipline slightly more manageable. The smartest approach is to anticipate that the part of your brain fixated on immediate gratification will resist when committing to a long-term task. Fortunately, with the right mindset and the tools discussed in the latter part of this book, this resistance can be overcome.

4

Chapter 3: The Power of Your Choices

In the vast tapestry of life, there are countless aspects beyond our control. We cannot select our parents or customize our genetic makeup to perfection. We cannot dictate how others treat us. However, within this realm of uncertainty, we possess a remarkable ability to shape our lives through the choices we make. This chapter delves into the concept that life is a continuous sequence of decisions. When viewed through the lens of options and their outcomes, the process of decision-making becomes more manageable and comprehensible.

When faced with a problem, a decision inevitably emerges: what action will you take? There is no escape from this choice. Even opting to abstain from making a decision is, in itself, a choice. By relinquishing control and allowing external factors or other people to decide on your behalf, you are still making a choice—a choice of passivity.

I recall a situation where I shared an office with a colleague unexpectedly. Initially, it was meant to be temporary, but as days turned into weeks, uncertainty loomed. Instead of resigning myself to the situation, I chose to work from home when feasible. Eventually, my coworker decided to leave the company, resolving the issue in my favor. Although this passive approach worked out well, it's not a recommended strategy. Taking charge of your decisions is vital for your autonomy and mental well-being.

CHAPTER 3: THE POWER OF YOUR CHOICES

To achieve a goal, you must actively select one discomfort over another. Consider the example of aspiring to write a novel. You face a decision: endure the challenges of dedicating time and effort to your writing, or suffer the regret of never pursuing your creative aspirations. Opting for the former means sacrificing leisure time, dealing with distractions, and justifying your choices to others. The alternative, however, leads to perpetual regret for abandoning your literary ambitions.

This perspective on life's choices might initially seem bleak. Yet, understanding that life comprises a series of decisions between various types of challenges can be empowering. Recognizing that your choices are based on the inevitable consequences of your actions restores a sense of control and purpose. It transforms you into a responsible adult who comprehends that life rarely offers easy answers and demands disciplined decisions to navigate its complexities.

The concept of locus of control, a term from psychology, becomes crucial here. It refers to your perception of what influences the events in your life and profoundly affects your reactions. Those with an external locus perceive life as something that merely happens to them, crediting external forces for their successes or failures. In contrast, individuals with an internal locus believe in their active role in shaping outcomes, attributing achievements to their efforts and intelligence.

Operating from an internal locus of control aligns seamlessly with self-discipline. This mindset instills the belief that your choices significantly impact your life, making it easier to stay disciplined and committed. While individuals with an external locus can lead fulfilling lives, coupling an internal locus with self-discipline enhances success and fulfillment. Your early life experiences shape your locus of control. If you learned that your efforts were rewarded, you're more likely to carry this mindset into adulthood.

If you find yourself operating from an external locus of control, the power to change lies within you. The human brain's plasticity allows for a shift in thinking. Cultivate the habit of evaluating the pros and cons of each choice, basing your decisions on their consequences. Whether at work or in personal relationships, this approach empowers you to take charge and shape your destiny. Remember, you always have the choice to transform your perspective and seize control of your life's narrative.

5

Chapter 4: Discovering the Genuine Purpose of Your Existence

Imagine someone stopping you in the street and questioning the fundamental purpose of your existence. Most people might mumble something about happiness or leaving a legacy. Some, driven by cynicism or a scientific mindset, might argue that life has no inherent purpose and is merely a result of evolution.

In this chapter, I'll delve into how successful individuals infuse their lives with genuine meaning and an enduring sense of purpose. It's not about conjuring infinite motivation, as you already know motivation alone isn't the key to discipline or contentment. This is about understanding the broader perspective, the ultimate question: what's the point? The world can seem harsh, especially in an age of constant news updates highlighting daily suffering, persistent inequalities, illness, and mortality. It's tempting to succumb to despair.

Unless you have unwavering faith in a specific religion or spiritual belief, you've likely grappled with the existential query of why you exist and how to make the most of your life. During our teenage years, many of us become cynical, questioning societal norms and rules, and seeking a higher purpose or vocation. However, as adulthood sets in, routine often takes over, and we suppress the urge to ponder the deeper meaning of our existence. Yet, as we enter our thirties or forties, the question of purpose resurfaces.

My own journey mirrored this pattern. After a seemingly ordinary upbringing, my parents' divorce during my teenage years left me bewildered. I fell into a period of depression, struggling to find meaning. Later, in my twenties, the question of purpose resurfaced, leading me to explore self-development and positive psychology. I wanted to understand why some people find meaning despite life's challenges.

I discovered two vital ways to infuse life with enduring purpose, creating a positive cycle. Both paths hinge on taking responsibility for your life and developing an internal locus of control, laying the groundwork for robust self-discipline.

The first route involves acknowledging and overcoming your internal weaknesses. This doesn't mean self-flagellation or comparison with others. Rather, it requires accepting your humanity, with a unique blend of strengths and weaknesses. Embrace your imperfections, for they provide the canvas for self-improvement and personal growth. You can't change others significantly, so invest your energy in self-improvement. Focus on fixing yourself first, gaining self-mastery, and becoming the best version of yourself. The respect earned from such personal transformation allows your influence to permeate the lives of those around you.

The second path involves conquering external limitations. Consider your idols; most likely, they've surmounted numerous obstacles. Challenges aren't personal attacks; they are universal experiences. Each external limitation is an opportunity to flex your self-discipline muscles, enhancing problem-solving skills, evaluating options, and choosing the best path based on your current knowledge and abilities. Life's difficulties aren't meant to be easy; they are the crucibles in which your discipline is honed, filling you with a profound and lasting sense of purpose.

6

Chapter 5: Discovering Your True Desires and How to Attain Them

If you were asked what people truly desire in life, what would come to mind? Wealth, good health, eternal life, physical attractiveness? According to media portrayals, we're all relentlessly pursuing fatter bank accounts, slimmer bodies, and public adoration.

But what if I proposed a different notion? What if we assumed that, above all else, what everyone craves is more control over their lives? Possessing immense wealth and material possessions means little if you perceive your life spiraling beyond your influence. Autonomy, the ability to steer your own journey, holds profound satisfaction.

When control slips through our fingers, panic often ensues.

Oddly enough, death isn't humanity's greatest fear. If it were, suicides wouldn't occur. What we truly cherish, often subconsciously, is the ability to exercise our judgment and make decisions. The feeling of power over our existence is paramount on a psychological level. Losing this control, our autonomy, constitutes our deepest, most significant fear.

Those who have experienced a panic attack understand the terror of losing control over their own bodies. Shortness of breath, waves of heat and cold, dizziness – panic attacks bring a feeling of losing one's sanity. Mental health issues and psychosis are feared because they signify a loss of control over emotions, thoughts, and reality.

External events that render us helpless can lead to tragic outcomes. Suicides and other tragedies often stem from individuals feeling trapped, especially in financial crises. The loss of control over one's life, like sudden financial ruin, can drive individuals to contemplate suicide, seeking permanent escape from their personal hell. Even assisted suicides often involve individuals fearing not death itself, but the agony of living their final days in pain and dependence.

Relationships, too, are sources of stress and helplessness. Placing one person at the center of your emotional world grants them immense power over your well-being. Yet, people frequently wonder why moving on becomes a struggle after the end of such relationships.

Reclaiming control over your life offers the best chance at achieving your desires and restoring your dignity. You won't feel at the mercy of random events or others' whims. Self-understanding and control are challenging enough; why complicate life further by attempting to control others?

Successful individuals grasp the significance of control. They aren't super-human; they understand that control begets momentum. Once you regain control in one area, it spills over into others. Committing to reclaiming control fosters a proactive attitude, creating a belief in your capabilities.

Allow me to illustrate this with a personal example. I used to detest the idea of working out. While I occasionally contemplated improving my physique for confidence, it wasn't sufficient to drive change. Then, my father suffered a stroke, and witnessing his struggle became a wake-up call. I vowed never to end up in a similar state. This led me to prioritize fitness, viewing it as a means to safeguard my health and ensure a strong recovery if necessary.

When setting new goals, ensure they increase your control over life. Starting a business to gain autonomy over your career and living situation is a powerful motive. To find fulfillment, eliminate hindrances and pursue joy.

I'd argue that control and self-mastery are the keys to happiness. In the next chapter, explore what truly brings contentment and how to sidestep common pitfalls in your pursuit of happiness.

Chapter 6: The Unexpected Reality of Happiness

What does true happiness entail, and is our contemporary idea of happiness the key to a fulfilling life? Just as people often view success as a singular event rather than a journey, many of us fall into the misconception that happiness is something that magically occurs when all conditions in our lives align perfectly. In this chapter, I will critically examine the concept of happiness and, more importantly, explain why self-discipline is the most dependable route to genuine contentment.

In today's Western culture, happiness is often equated with the quantity of material possessions we own and the level of social status we attain. Wealthy celebrities with legions of fans are held up as role models, regardless of their actual achievements. We are taught to believe that a happy life demands minimal effort yet offers an endless stream of pleasure. The notion that those who can afford a leisurely life, devoid of work-related constraints, are the happiest is pervasive. However, research reveals that once you earn enough to cover basic needs like food and shelter, the correlation between material wealth and happiness weakens.

It might surprise you to know that people in the past didn't view a life filled with pleasure and minimal effort as the path to fulfillment. Our contemporary definition of happiness as the avoidance of pain, along with the pursuit of pleasure and safety, emerged only in the 18th century—a relatively recent development in human history. If you could travel back in time and ask an ancient Greek about this definition of happiness, they would find it absurd.

In the past, happiness carried different implications; it was about accomplishment, competition, and pride in developing virtues like generosity and self-control. Self-discipline was considered the key to happiness, and hard work was esteemed. No one aspired to idleness. People found satisfaction in overcoming their weaknesses and striving toward higher ideals, often enduring challenges along the way. These concepts echo the importance of prioritizing long-term results over instant gratification and dedicating time to self-improvement.

Our perspective on suffering has also shifted over the years. Many Westerners mistakenly believe that happiness should be accessible to all, without suffering. Suffering is seen as the antithesis of happiness, rather than an inherent part of life. We fear suffering, and some of us feel so entitled to a "good life" that we question why we should endure anything that hinders our desires.

Terminal illness and death remain some of the last societal taboos in the West. We avoid acknowledging our humanity and the numerous limitations it brings. Society is fixated on maintaining youthfulness and avoids confronting mortality at all costs. Even during funerals, euphemisms like "passed on" are used, revealing our discomfort with acknowledging the harsh realities of life and death.

Yet, suffering is natural; the wisest among us have recognized this for centuries. Buddhism, for instance, teaches us to accept pain and discomfort as unavoidable aspects of life. Paradoxically, the greater our acceptance, the happier we become. To grasp this teaching fully, it's essential to understand the two types of suffering.

The first type is necessary suffering—unavoidable aspects of human existence like loss, illness, and natural disasters. The second type is unnecessary suffering, stemming from rumination, procrastination, and avoidance of confronting problems. This suffering is self-generated. How we react to what happens to us affects our mental state.

For instance, falling ill with the flu involves necessary suffering, as you must wait for the symptoms to pass. However, if you dwell on the activities missed due to illness, your suffering becomes unnecessary. Procrastination is another form of unnecessary suffering. It often arises from fear, which, in turn, is linked to anxiety when things are beyond our control. Procrastination worsens situations, yet we engage in it to avoid pain or discomfort, inadvertently intensifying our suffering.

The common thread in these scenarios is our belief that we shouldn't experience suffering at all. However, if we acknowledge that fear and suffering are inevitable and make the sensible choice—to endure suffering now rather than intensify it later—we can find happiness.

Another misconception is viewing happiness as an all-or-nothing state, where we expect to feel only positive emotions and lack negative ones like sadness or uncertainty. This belief leads to the common Western scenario where we wonder why we can't "just be happy" despite having secure homes, clean water, and continuous entertainment.

We forget our humanity, allowing room for negative emotions alongside gratitude and happiness. Our moods fluctuate due to various factors beyond our control, and sometimes we must accept that not everything needs an explanation. By prioritizing self-discipline, these day-to-day fluctuations become inconsequential. You remain focused on meeting your goals and obligations.

At this point, the limitations of our Western ideas about suffering and happiness should be evident. We can't hope to attain happiness by evading all suffering because some of it is inevitable. True happiness comes when we manage to avoid unnecessary suffering. How do we achieve this? Through self-discipline! Self-discipline empowers you to be as happy as a person can reasonably be, considering the inevitable obstacles in life. Moreover, good self-discipline enables you to find enjoyment and pride in overcoming setbacks. Facing the reality of suffering with bravery, and accepting it as inevitable, allows you to maintain a rational, balanced view of life. In this perspective, happiness becomes an experience to be cherished but never taken for granted.

8

Chapter 7: Harnessing the Power of Optimism

We've all heard that maintaining a positive attitude can boost happiness and productivity, but it's crucial to approach positivity in the right manner. Positive thinking can indeed aid in achieving your goals, but it must be coupled with proactive steps; otherwise, your life won't change significantly.

In this chapter, we'll explore how you can benefit from a positive mindset without relying on unrealistic optimism or blind faith. Throughout this book, I've emphasized the importance of staying rooted in reality. There's no magic solution, quick-fix course, or flawless self-help book that can replace the work you need to put in. Ultimately, your success in life rests on your shoulders. It's about finding a balance between contemplation and action.

As humans, we are always focusing on something. How we choose to direct our attention profoundly impacts our emotions, self-discipline, and drive. Even individuals with ADHD focus, albeit switching rapidly from one thing to another. Therefore, it's vital to be mindful of where you direct your attention. A practical starting point is to focus on what you have rather than what you lack. You can practice this through a gratitude exercise. Every morning or evening, spend a few minutes reflecting on the positive aspects of your life.

Write them down; this exercise enhances self-discipline and deepens your engagement with positive thinking and gratitude. Your list doesn't need to be extraordinary; being thankful for basic necessities like running water and a bed is enough. Consider maintaining a diary where you focus on positive situations, emotions, and experiences rather than dwelling on negative events.

If you don't actively focus on the good, you'll naturally start concentrating on the bad. Humans can't concentrate on nothing at all; thus, you have a choice—focus on what's going well or what's going wrong. Negativity fosters helplessness and depression, hindering your progress. Conversely, developing a habit of concentrating on the positives nurtures a mindset that sees the world as a realm of exciting opportunities.

However, it's essential to note that positive thinking is not a substitute for real action. Beware of positive thinking philosophies that promote laziness, such as the "Law Of Attraction" (LOA). While LOA can provide inspiration, it shouldn't trick you into believing that great results will come without effort. Practical tools like visualization and affirmations can be effective. Affirmations, stated in the present tense and positively, create a mental image of your desired situation. Repeat them daily and visualize your goal with intensity, engaging all your senses. When combined with a practical plan and determination, affirmations and visualization become powerful tools. But it's crucial to know precisely how to achieve your goals; otherwise, positive thinking won't lead to tangible changes.

It's important to understand that positive thinking isn't a cure-all. Even the most positive people encounter suffering; it's an inevitable part of life. Situations can be genuinely challenging, and positive thinking might not alleviate your pain. Allow yourself to feel sadness or regret, then focus on the future.

Regarding failure, it's essential not to ignore it but to learn from it. Analyze what went wrong and consider how to improve next time. Successful individuals don't wallow in self-pity; they acknowledge their mistakes, learn, and move forward. You can train yourself to think differently, even in the face of failure. Positive self-deception, where you convince yourself that the mistake never happened, can be a powerful method to overcome past failures.

However, it's possible to overemphasize positivity and lose touch with your emotions. Suppressing genuine feelings like frustration, anger, or despair can deprive you of vital motivators for change. Negative emotions, though painful, can fuel lasting transformations. They act as a real-life motivator, driving you toward meaningful change.

Misused, positive thinking can also lead you to avoid practical action to prevent situations from worsening. Some problems require confrontation; ignoring them may exacerbate the issues. Recognize what you can let go of and what requires immediate attention. Confronting life with a positive outlook generally benefits you now and in the future. Remember, facing challenges head-on, with optimism and practicality, can lead to enduring solutions.

9

Chapter 8: Embracing Failure for Success

How does the mere mention of "failure" make you feel? For many, the very thought of it is more terrifying than death itself. In this chapter, I challenge you to reconsider your relationship with failure and even embrace it. We'll explore why we dread failure, why it's okay to make mistakes, and what valuable lessons can be gleaned from our missteps.

Our fear of failure stems from two primary sources. Firstly, it relates to the loss of control. Regardless of our personality types, we all prefer a sense of predictability in life. Unexpected events throw us off balance, even when they seem positive, like winning the lottery or falling in love unexpectedly. Every goal carries the inherent risk of failure, leaving us uncertain about the outcome and our emotional response to success or failure.

The second reason revolves around societal conditioning. From our early years in kindergarten, we're bombarded with the notion that failure is the worst thing that can happen. Paradoxically, we learn through failure, especially during our formative years when we learn to walk, talk, and perform basic tasks. However, as we progress through school, the tolerance for failure diminishes. Parents and teachers become less forgiving, creating an environment where failure is stigmatized. This fear of failure often paralyzes individuals, preventing them from pursuing their true potential and settling for mediocrity.

This fear often hampers our ability to take risks and explore new opportunities. We might dream of a fulfilling life, envisioning ideal careers or self-employment, but fear creeps in. Doubts arise: "What if I fail in a new field? What if I can't find clients? What if I'm not good enough?" These anxieties can consume us, leading to rumination and exhaustion. However, acknowledging that the fear won't vanish magically is the first step. You can either succumb to fear and stagnate or accept it and take the leap despite the apprehension.

The simplest way to evade failure is by doing nothing. If you're convinced you can't handle any setbacks, remaining in your comfort zone and avoiding risks might seem appealing. Yet, every choice in life has a price. Avoiding challenges comes at a high cost; you risk regretting missed opportunities and unfulfilled ambitions. Risks inject life with adrenaline and purpose, enhancing personal development. Failure is inevitable; accepting it is the key to growth.

Failure, however, doesn't define your worth or competence. It's a result of countless variables beyond your control and the limitations you work within. Crucially, failure must not be taken personally. External factors, like a sudden economic downturn, can derail the best-laid plans. The crucial factor is how you respond to failure. Your response depends on your perception of the situation.

Consider the placebo effect: beliefs have power. Likewise, your perception of failure shapes your reality. Many view failures as confirmation of their deepest fears: that they aren't good enough or that hard work never leads to success. This negative mindset becomes a self-fulfilling prophecy, eroding self-discipline and pushing success further away.

However, there's a healthier way to respond to failure. The most successful individuals anticipate and welcome failure as valuable feedback. Each failure provides essential data about what doesn't work, guiding them toward the right path. Notable figures across various fields, including renowned author Stephen King, have faced multiple rejections before achieving remarkable success. Failure isn't the antithesis of success; it's an integral part of it. Each failure, when embraced and persevered through, strengthens your resilience and determination. Failure becomes a stepping stone, not an endpoint.

Remember, every failure is an opportunity to learn, grow, and become better equipped for future challenges. Failure isn't a dead end; it's a detour on the road to success. By acknowledging your failures and learning from them, you build not only your practical skills but also your inner strength. In the end, you'll appreciate the obstacles you encountered on your journey toward ultimate success.

At this point, you might intellectually agree with this perspective on failure, yet still, find it challenging to fully accept. In the next chapter, I'll introduce you to a philosophy that helped me reconcile with the idea that not everything is within our control.

10

Chapter 9: Harnessing Zen Philosophy for Goal Achievement

Imagine living a life where you effortlessly navigate through challenges, unburdened by the anxiety of impending changes. Picture yourself free from the constant fear of not doing enough with your life and at peace with the inevitability of mortality. In this chapter, we delve into an ancient philosophy, rooted in Buddhist teachings and focused on Zen principles, that has enriched Eastern lives for centuries. You're about to discover how embracing Zen philosophy can enhance your self-discipline and propel you closer to your goals.

Now, don't worry, this won't turn into a tedious lecture. Zen has been extensively explored in numerous books, including my own. It encompasses various schools of thought, but you don't need to delve deep into scholarly pursuits to benefit from its wisdom. You don't have to adopt Buddhism, engage in lengthy morning meditations, or don orange robes. What you do need is to grasp a few fundamental concepts to fortify your self-discipline.

Researchers in psychology and self-development have observed that Zen practitioners often enjoy robust psychological well-being. Studies from Penn State University highlight the positive impact of Zen practices, such as meditation, on stress reduction, inducing calmness, and enhancing decision-making abilities.

Zen philosophy, often referred to as "satori" in Japanese, translates to a "flash of inspiration" or a "first showing." It's not a religion but a way of life based on Buddha's teachings. To experience Zen is to live fully in the present, recognizing the interconnectedness of all things. Achieving this state involves a suspension of the self and ego, a state challenging to articulate but transformative in its essence.

To grasp Zen, it's helpful to understand Buddha's teachings. He emphasized two key concepts: the inherent presence of suffering in human life and the self-inflicted nature of this suffering. Buddha ventured into the world to learn about existence and observed that people often dwell in misery due to their attachments and illusions. These attachments include our sense of self, which, in reality, is a construct created by our minds. The aim of Buddhism, particularly Zen, is to dispel these illusions and recognize the interconnected nature of existence. With this insight, societal concerns like social status and material possessions lose significance. Instead, emphasis shifts to moral development and a balanced life, freeing individuals from the delusion that external events dictate their happiness.

Buddhism advocates living in the present moment, dismissing past memories as mere interpretations and future worries as sources of pointless mental suffering. Zen principles challenge rigid self-identities, encouraging detachment from self-imposed limitations. Holding tightly to predefined notions of who we are restricts personal growth and fosters destructive behavioral patterns. For instance, identifying solely as a high achiever might lead to stress and burnout, as constant success becomes an unrelenting expectation. Incorporating Zen principles can help break free from such constraints, promoting mental well-being and balanced self-perception.

By accepting the inevitability of suffering and embracing the present, you cultivate self-discipline. Zen philosophy helps you gain control over your mind, preventing wasteful rumination and regrets, allowing you to focus on appreciating the current moment. The practice of meditation, often advocated in Buddhism, aids in achieving this mental discipline, a topic we will explore in the next chapter. Additionally, living in the present diminishes fear, freeing you from the constraints of negative thoughts and empowering sharper thinking and calmness.

You might wonder if this focus on the present leaves any room for setting and pursuing goals. Contrary to this concern, Buddhism, including Zen, offers proactive guidelines within the framework of the Eightfold Path, which includes directives like "right speech," "right view," and "right action." These guidelines are inherently proactive and goal-oriented, illustrating that Zen principles and goal-oriented living can coexist harmoniously.

Living in the present provides an additional advantage: it prevents feeling overwhelmed by long-term goals. Focusing on small, incremental steps rather than a distant end result curbs feelings of inadequacy and dread associated with daunting journeys.

So, how can you incorporate Zen principles into your mindset and actions? In the upcoming chapter, we'll explore how some of the most disciplined individuals on the planet utilize Buddhist principles to achieve extraordinary goals, guiding you toward possibilities you might have never imagined.

11

Chapter 10: Embracing Self-Discipline the Shaolin Way

Now that you have a grasp of the fundamental Zen principles and their application, let's explore how these concepts translate into practical, real-life scenarios. In this chapter, we will delve into the lives of a remarkable group of Buddhist monks – the Shaolin. By delving into their daily routines and beliefs, you will gain insight into how adhering to the principles discussed in the previous chapter can pave the way for a disciplined life. Interestingly, Shaolin monks not only achieve extraordinary self-discipline but also enjoy a profound sense of well-being and inner peace. Their lifestyle has become a source of inspiration for many in the Western world.

But who are these exceptional individuals? The Shaolin Monastery in China stands as one of the most renowned Zen Buddhist temples globally, with a history dating back approximately 1500 years. According to legend, it was founded when a Buddhist teacher named Buddhabhadra journeyed from India to China. Buddhabhadra's innovative idea was to transmit Buddhism's core teachings directly from a master to a student, moving away from reliance on scriptures and written interpretations. Impressed by this concept, the Chinese Emperor provided funds for the construction of a new temple. These monks were not only spiritual practitioners but also became renowned for their martial arts prowess, mastering over 70 specialized techniques, including the famous "Iron Head" maneuver. Some monks even travel globally, showcasing their extraordinary skills to large audiences.

Today, despite historical attacks and demolitions, the temple still houses monks celebrated for their mastery of kung fu. Their day begins at 5 am and concludes at 11 pm, revolving around three main activities – studying Buddhism, practicing kung fu, and engaging in essential temple duties like cleaning and food preparation. Each monk dedicates significant hours daily to rigorous physical exercise, coupled with intense mental and spiritual training. Their lifestyle advocates minimal material possessions and external interests. Upon joining the temple, each monk shaves their head, symbolizing their allegiance to Buddha's teachings and their willingness to relinquish material attachments.

How do they maintain the rigorous discipline required to adhere to such a stringent schedule? According to Matthew Ahmet, a British-born monk who trained at the temple, the Shaolin embrace attitudes remarkably different from those prevalent in the West. Firstly, they live with basic facilities, washing clothes by hand and lacking running water, fostering gratitude for life's simplest aspects. This gratitude provides a positive foundation – appreciating small things builds psychological momentum, instilling a belief in a fundamentally good world abundant with opportunities, propelling them toward their goals.

Secondly, the monks understand that material possessions and wealth don't guarantee happiness. They don't envy those leading conventional lives, realizing that genuine contentment comes from discovering a passion or mission. For them, it's the spiritual and physical progress made during their temple training. This lesson underscores a simple yet profound truth – aligning your goals with your values and ambitions fuels enduring passion. Even amidst challenges and seeming endless journeys, a sense of purpose sustains self-discipline.

Thirdly, they avoid pushing themselves to the point of pain or injury. Historically, monks needed to be fit for potential temple attacks. They believed that an ill or injured monk resulting from excessive physical or mental exertion would be ineffective in battle. This principle still guides modern monks. Although they engage in extensive physical training daily, they incorporate rest periods, acknowledging that busyness doesn't equate to productivity. Recognizing the need to balance hard work with downtime, meditation becomes crucial. It reduces mental clutter, enhances psychological resilience, and teaches the harmony between intense effort and relaxation.

Meditation is central to their routine. Kung fu practitioners emphasize emotional regulation and avoiding negative impulses. To fight effectively, mastering their life force, known as "chi" in the Shaolin tradition, is vital. Monks train not only in high-energy kung fu but also in tai chi, a slow martial art requiring intense concentration and balance. Tai chi teaches combatants to remain aware and focused, enabling swift and effective strikes. Shaolin monks attribute their remarkable physical resilience to this mastery of chi. After years of training, a typical Shaolin monk can endure blows that would prove fatal to others, redirecting and repelling attacks with their energy control.

Additionally, meditation aids in self-discovery, enabling a strong connection with one's true self. This introspection fuels their vigor, driving them toward physical, mental, and spiritual excellence. For the Shaolin, meditation isn't a single practice but a continuous state of mindfulness, fostering sustained concentration.

Interestingly, the Shaolin's approach aligns with the discipline exhibited by Navy SEALs. Both groups share unwavering commitment to their respective causes, displaying immense self-discipline and a willingness to sacrifice comforts for greater goals. Similar to SEALs, the monks don't solely rely on motivation; they rely on strong ideals and strict routines, cultivating a sense of momentum. This steadfast commitment, coupled with a sense of purpose, propels them forward.

CHAPTER 10: EMBRACING SELF-DISCIPLINE THE SHAOLIN WAY

Despite their distinctive lifestyle, the Shaolin monks share a common habit with productive individuals – adhering to a daily routine. In the upcoming part of this book, an entire chapter is dedicated to crafting effective schedules that enhance self-discipline. However, before diving into that, we will explore another practical skill derived from the Shaolin tradition – meditation. Flip to the next chapter to learn how this ancient spiritual tool can be integrated into your life right now.

II

Part: 2

12

Chapter 11: Cultivating Focus and Self-Discipline through Meditation

The preceding chapter likely convinced you of the tremendous impact regular meditation can have on enhancing your self-discipline. If it can yield remarkable results for Shaolin monks, consider the potential it holds for you! In this chapter, I will guide you through basic exercises that will empower you to master the art of meditation. If you've ever dismissed meditation as dull or a waste of time, get ready to challenge those assumptions.

Firstly, you don't need to spend hours sitting to meditate effectively. Similar to Shaolin monks, who view meditation as a lifestyle, you must adopt a comparable mindset. While a regular practice is beneficial, the true power of meditation shines when life's daily stresses become more manageable. Let's explore why and how meditation can benefit you.

Meditation amplifies your ability to make rational decisions and maintain focus. It transforms you into an expert at delaying immediate gratification for long-term goals, a key element of self-discipline. Daily hassles won't vanish, but meditation equips you with a calm, rational outlook, enabling you to respond to setbacks with resilience.

Doubting the efficacy of meditation? Scientific evidence supports it. A study published in PNAS demonstrated significant improvements in attention, reduced fatigue, lower stress, and decreased anxiety in participants after just five days of 20-minute daily meditation sessions. Imagine the productivity boost when you feel more energized and in control of your thoughts! Even on days when motivation is lacking, meditation imparts skills essential for self-discipline.

Here's how to start. Begin with a seated meditation. Find a comfortable position—cross-legged on the floor or in a chair with an upright posture. Ensure your back is straight but relaxed, mouth closed, and eyes softly focused about two feet ahead.

The essence of meditation lies in focusing your mind. Two techniques are effective. First, concentrate on your breathing, feeling the air moving in through your nose and out through your mouth. Deep, abdominal breathing ensures proper oxygen flow, vital for overall health. The second technique, known as "Shikantaza" or "just sitting," involves observing your thoughts without judgment. Treat your thoughts like passing clouds, accepting them before letting go. This practice promotes a healthier attitude toward negative thoughts in everyday life, freeing you from self-deprecation.

During meditation, your mind might wander. When it does, gently bring your focus back to the present. Don't chastise yourself; meditation skills improve with practice, offering a calmer, more controlled life.

If sitting still proves challenging or if anxiety impedes your thoughts, try walking meditation. Known as "Kinhin," it offers a dynamic alternative. Stand barefoot, maintaining an upright posture and even weight distribution. With hands folded, focus on your breath, taking a step forward with each inhalation and exhalation. This slow practice cultivates self-control, fostering a proactive mental attitude crucial for success.

Consistency matters more than duration. Start with a few minutes and gradually increase. Personally, I meditate for 20 minutes twice daily, but your practice should align with your comfort level and schedule. Remember, meditation isn't negotiable—it's an essential part of your self-care routine, a testament to your commitment to personal growth. In the next chapter, you'll understand why the concept of "trying" can hinder your progress.

13

Chapter 12: Embracing Action Over Attempt

One of the most straightforward yet profoundly impactful steps you can take right now to enhance your self-discipline is to eliminate a single word from your vocabulary. This small change can transform how you perceive yourself and significantly boost your self-esteem. Your thoughts and the words you use, both aloud and in your mind, shape your self-image and, ultimately, your success.

So, which word should you remove? Starting today, banish the word "try." In this chapter, you'll learn why allowing yourself to "try" instead of committing to action holds you back from your goals and undermines your self-discipline. Despite its size, "try" can create substantial problems for you.

As children, many of us were encouraged to try our best. Well-meaning adults reassured us that putting in effort mattered, regardless of the outcome. Phrases like "It's not the winning, but the taking part that counts" reinforced this mindset. While this sentiment is comforting, it doesn't always hold true in real life. Opportunities can be fleeting, requiring you to seize the moment. From now on, you won't try; you will simply DO. If you find yourself saying "I'll try," stop and say "I will do" instead. Be courageous and decisive in your

CHAPTER 12: EMBRACING ACTION OVER ATTEMPT

speech and actions. This change not only earns self-respect but also shapes others' perceptions of you. It positions you as a proactive achiever rather than someone who fears failure and does nothing.

Trying leaves room for ambiguity, making it easier for you to evade accountability. When you aim to try, you allow yourself too much flexibility. How hard do you need to try before you can claim you gave your all? It's hard to measure, leaving you susceptible to self-deception. In contrast, DOING is clear and evident—you either accomplish the task or you don't. No excuses are acceptable. Trust in your abilities and face your strengths and weaknesses honestly. This self-discipline involves self-assessment and the courage to confront your true self. If you believe you can succeed, act on it. Proper planning is vital. Clarify your goals, assess your chances of success, and take decisive action. Doing is assertive and unequivocal, unlike the uncertain nature of trying.

Choosing to try focuses your attention on limitations and obstacles, fostering negative beliefs that hinder your progress. For instance, if you say you'll try to lose weight, you're setting yourself up for a struggle. Instead, focus on DOING, which emphasizes possibilities over obstacles. Failure, though daunting, is not the end; it's a chance to learn. Trying doesn't build character; taking action and learning from results do.

Successful people understand that to achieve anything, they must assume they will succeed and continually push themselves. They act instead of merely trying. For example, renowned self-development expert Deepak Chopra advises, "Don't try. Do."

To make this mental shift, strengthen your self-belief. Set achievable goals and remind yourself daily that you will DO them. Establish habits and routines that lead to success, transforming you from a "tryer" into a doer. In the next chapter, discover why winning and losing are habits and how you can set yourself firmly on the path to consistent victory with a few simple rules.

14

Chapter 13: The Essential Principles of Achievement

Life, essentially, is a training ground. To maximize your potential, view life as a dynamic, ever-changing experience demanding discipline and self-awareness. Even after reaching your goals, standing still leads to a loss of momentum. It all boils down to the choices you make. You are continually training yourself, either towards a winning or a losing mindset. Taking responsibility for your life direction is crucial. In this chapter, we'll explore five fundamental rules that can empower you to excel in any endeavor.

These rules are universally applicable, whether you aim to boost efficiency at work, foster healthier relationships, or shed some weight. Once mastered, these principles will skyrocket your productivity and self-belief. They serve as a framework promoting self-discipline and accountability. While challenging, embracing these rules is profoundly rewarding. As you read, contemplate how these principles can be applied to your current goals.

The first rule is clarity in your desires. Before embarking on any project, answer two vital questions. First, can you articulate precisely what you want? A detailed vision enhances your chances of success. For instance, compare "I want to lose 15lbs" with "I plan to lose 15lbs, double my gym lifting capacity, and buy three new outfits by the end of July!" The latter, being more specific and emotional, is inspiring. Your goal should also align with your core values, giving you purpose. Recognize the sacrifices you'll need to make and evaluate whether the goal is worth the effort.

The second rule emphasizes a direct approach. People who merely "try" often attempt multiple methods, investing minimal effort due to a fear of failure. This inefficiency is counterproductive. Clarify your steps, double-check details, and commit to your plan. A well-thought-out plan acts as a guiding light during challenges, reminding you of your realistic goals.

The third rule emphasizes small, consistent steps. Oddly, taking small steps requires as much discipline as giant leaps. Initial enthusiasm can lead to burnout. A steady, measured pace, documented in a logbook, promotes disciplined progress and builds your self-discipline.

The fourth rule stresses repetition. Mastering a skill, like learning a language, requires identifying effective exercises and drills, committing to them daily, and persisting through occasional frustration. The key is to repeat exercises consistently, even on uninspired days.

The final rule underscores celebrating small victories. Break daunting goals into manageable sub-goals. Celebrate each achievement, reinforcing your sense of victory. Maintaining a positive attitude and self-image is pivotal. By viewing yourself as a winner, consistent action becomes the path to triumph.

In the pursuit of your goals, focus on the process. Understanding the importance of enjoying the journey is crucial. Appreciating the hard work required fortifies your determination. In the next chapter, you'll learn why relishing the pursuit of a goal is vital for sustained motivation.

Chapter 14: Embracing the Journey

Once you've defined your goal and figured out the necessary steps to reach it, the next crucial move is to find pleasure in the process. Why? Relying solely on motivation or sheer determination won't sustain you for long. In this chapter, I'll guide you on how to genuinely enjoy the hard work essential for unlocking your full potential.

We've explored the limitations of motivation before. While focusing on a goal can be motivating, the day-to-day grind involved in achieving it can drain your energy unless you learn to find fulfillment in the work itself. Luckily, understanding basic psychology can help you look forward to the journey as much as the destination.

Consider the power of association, as demonstrated by Ivan Pavlov's famous experiments with dogs. Pavlov found that by pairing a sound (like a bell ringing) with food, he could make the dogs salivate at the sound alone. This principle applies to humans too. By linking positive feelings to difficult tasks, you can learn to enjoy them. For example, when working on a daunting project, create positive associations by enjoying your favorite drink, reading an inspiring article, or listening to calming ambient noises. Reward yourself after completing tasks, strengthening the connection between hard work and positive emotions.

CHAPTER 14: EMBRACING THE JOURNEY

Additionally, tap into your sense of identity. Visualize the person you're becoming through this process. If you're training for a marathon, see yourself as a healthy, energetic individual unafraid of physical challenges. This mental shift can transform your perspective from seeing the journey as a slog to viewing it as an exciting period of growth.

Gratitude is another powerful mindset. Appreciate the opportunity you have to change your life through your efforts. Celebrate small achievements, even with symbolic gestures like gold stars on a calendar. These simple acts reinforce the rewarding nature of the process.

Recognize that every successful person has faced grueling hours of work. Avoid comparing your private struggles with others' public successes. Understanding that hard work is part of the journey can fortify your determination. Embrace the challenges, knowing they are stepping stones toward your goals.

Furthermore, train yourself to resist distractions and temptations that could derail your progress. In the next chapter, we'll delve into scientific research on temptation and strategies to delay gratification.

16

Chapter 15: Mastering Patience and Resisting Temptation

Learning to delay gratification and resist the allure of instant results is a vital skill for building self-discipline. Once you become adept at prioritizing long-term goals over immediate desires, your chances of achieving success significantly increase. In this chapter, I'll share some straightforward techniques to strengthen your self-control, delay gratification, and fend off temptations. Keep in mind that while these methods are simple, they aren't necessarily easy. Similar to a muscle, self-control improves with practice. The more you train yourself to delay rewards, the easier it becomes. This heightened self-discipline not only helps you stay focused on long-term projects but also prevents distractions like the internet from sidetracking you.

We've all encountered individuals with unwavering focus, as well as those who struggle to concentrate on any project due to wandering attention. Research, such as Walter Mischel's iconic marshmallow test over 40 years ago, demonstrates that self-control tendencies often appear early in life. In the test, preschoolers were offered a choice: wait for a researcher's return and receive two marshmallows or ring a bell for immediate gratification with just one marshmallow. Follow-ups with these children revealed that those who resisted instant rewards in preschool exhibited higher grades, greater stress resilience, enhanced concentration, and better self-control into middle age.

While genetic factors might influence self-control, brain plasticity offers hope for those with impulsive tendencies. The brain's ability to change means you can alter your behavior, which, in turn, reshapes your brain. Commit to delaying rewards, and this practice will become easier over time. Start with small changes, like waiting twenty minutes before indulging in a coffee or delaying opening a message on your phone for five minutes. Acknowledge your efforts each time you resist temptation, reinforcing the positive feeling associated with self-control. Denying yourself momentarily can become gratifying, especially when compared to the fleeting satisfaction of giving in.

Once you've mastered short delays for minor rewards, challenge yourself with longer intervals. Instead of minutes or hours, think in terms of days. For instance, if you desire a new shirt, decide to buy it only if you can wait a week. Often, by the end of the seven days, your initial urge would have faded, making the purchase seem unnecessary. Regularly practicing these exercises trains your mind to excel at delaying gratification. Moreover, it reshapes your self-image, portraying you as someone capable of making wise decisions and sacrificing momentary desires for long-term goals.

Understanding the crucial role of self-image in achieving success and lasting change is essential. Our actions often align with our self-perception, whether it holds us back or propels us forward. Affirmations and visualization, combined with the regular practice of delaying gratification, significantly enhance our efforts. By repeating empowering statements like "I have great self-control" and visualizing the satisfaction of mastering temptation, we reinforce our self-discipline.

Additionally, stress and fatigue impact decision-making abilities. Psychological research emphasizes the depletion of willpower as the day progresses. To navigate this, it's wise to tackle important decisions and challenging tasks early in the day when willpower is strongest. Save enjoyable activities for later, capitalizing on the natural energy dip in the afternoon. This approach not only aids productivity but also boosts momentum and a sense of accomplishment.

Blood sugar levels also influence our ability to resist temptation. Stable glucose levels are essential for clear thinking and wise choices. To enhance self-control, maintain consistent blood sugar levels by consuming balanced meals and snacks regularly. Avoid prolonged periods of hunger, as it can lead to irritability and diminished concentration. Planning a sensible diet contributes significantly to productivity.

Everyday decisions, seemingly insignificant, shape our lives over time. Developing the skill of resisting temptation is crucial for achieving long-term goals. Each day presents an opportunity to exercise restraint, honing our ability to make choices that align with our ambitions. Taking these choices seriously transforms every area of our lives, guiding us toward success.

17

Chapter 16: Harnessing Negative Emotions for Success

Regardless of your positive outlook or preparation for success, moments of despair, sadness, anger, and frustration are inevitable aspects of the human experience. Many of us tend to avoid negative emotions, striving to quickly return to a state of happiness or at least contentment. In this chapter, I propose that embracing negative emotions is not only healthy but also can serve as potent fuel for self-control and reinforcing your sense of purpose.

Accepting the inevitability of suffering equips you to utilize your unpleasant emotions constructively. Rather than viewing negative feelings as inconveniences to be resolved swiftly, consider them as valuable signposts indicating necessary changes in your life. Instead of suppressing discomfort, transform it into motivation for action, aligning your thoughts and analysis with concrete steps.

Anger and rage, often difficult to manage, can be channeled positively. Rather than viewing anger as a loss of control or a means of manipulation, utilize its energy. Redirect it into physical activities like intense workouts or channel it toward long-term goals, such as proving your worth and overcoming obstacles. Envy, too, can be beneficial, signaling unmet desires and providing clear goals.

Analyze your envy, identify your desires, and use it as a foundation to build a plan for your own achievements.

Anxiety, despite its immobilizing potential, can be harnessed for success. Conquering fears brings immense satisfaction, serving as a motivator for overcoming challenges. Fear can also prompt constructive action, leading you to explore new opportunities or consider alternative paths. Make a list of strategies to handle feared outcomes, transforming fear into creative problem-solving.

Despair and sadness, though challenging, can be the foundation for self-discipline and accomplishment. Major life events like a difficult divorce or the loss of a close friend trigger self-reflection, enabling you to differentiate between vital life aspects and trivial pursuits. Focusing on meaningful goals becomes easier, redirecting your efforts toward worthwhile pursuits. By recognizing what truly matters, your ability to maintain self-discipline and manage your time improves, guiding you toward your objectives.

Have you ever come across an inspiring tale of someone achieving a significant goal in memory of a loved one? Many individuals find that their worst moments, like losing a partner to illness, can unexpectedly fuel their success. A common example is people transforming from sedentary lifestyles to marathon runners, driven by the desire to raise funds for a meaningful cause. Despite lacking prior athletic interests, their motivation to contribute in someone's memory reshapes their priorities. Some individuals become dedicated campaigners following tragic events, showcasing how negative emotions can be channeled positively.

For those pursuing creative goals, such as writing a novel or enhancing artistic skills, research indicates that negativity can be a catalyst. A study by Ghent University revealed that creative professionals were most productive on days when they woke up in a bad mood. This suggests that negative feelings can be directly converted into creative output. Engaging in artistic activities during moments of anger or sadness can be a constructive approach.

Shame, a powerful and debilitating emotion, often hinders personal growth. Unlike guilt, which signifies a recognition of wrongdoing, shame goes deeper, damaging self-worth. Overcoming shame is crucial for developing self-discipline. In her book "Daring Greatly," author Brene Brown provides guidance on how to address shame. Opening up to someone supportive can facilitate self-forgiveness, leading to acceptance and compassion. Letting go of shame allows for personal growth, enabling you to focus on your goals without the burden of self-criticism. Embrace these emotions as opportunities to adopt a more realistic perspective and cultivate a positive self-image, enabling you to pursue success with renewed determination.

18

Chapter 17: Sturgeon's Law & The Pareto Principle

Have you ever felt disheartened when your hard work doesn't yield the desired results? This chapter delves into the reasons why it's natural to invest hours, days, or even years into a project and still feel stuck. More importantly, it reveals how embracing this simple truth can empower you and enhance your self-discipline. We'll explore two concepts that will revolutionize your approach to work – Sturgeon's Law and the Pareto Principle.

In 1958, science fiction writer Theodore Sturgeon addressed the criticism that science fiction was of low quality. He argued that the claim that 90% of science fiction was "crap" applied to nearly everything else too. This insight, now known as Sturgeon's Law, remains influential in critical thinking today. Additionally, the Pareto Principle, formulated by Italian economist Vilfredo Pareto in 1896, states that 20% of efforts often yield 80% of results. This principle, also known as the 80/20 rule, is widely applied in various fields.

You might wonder why invest time and effort if there's a high chance your work won't meet expectations. If 90% of what you produce might not be great, why bother at all? The Pareto Principle suggests that only 20% of your efforts will bring significant results, which might seem discouraging.

However, these theories offer essential lessons, emphasizing the importance of self-discipline.

Firstly, they teach us that it's normal to work hard without knowing what will succeed. For instance, imagine you're an author releasing four novels. Three might not gain much traction, but one becomes a massive hit. Without understanding the Pareto Principle, you might feel disheartened. However, acknowledging this principle allows you to maintain realistic expectations, preventing isolated successes or failures from derailing your progress.

Accepting that only a fraction of your work will truly matter becomes a driving force to work smart and tirelessly. It gives you a reason to experiment with different approaches. Successful CEOs grasp this concept, taking risks on new products while persevering through failures. They recognize that consistent success is rare, and the best defense against disappointment is anticipating challenges. Embracing Sturgeon's Law and the Pareto Principle can fuel your resilience and foster the self-discipline needed to navigate your path effectively.

Chapter 18: Embracing Reality for Lasting Success

The 80/20 principle holds an intriguing perspective when viewed through the right lens. Although 80% of your endeavors might not yield the desired outcomes, that remaining 20% possesses the potential to drive you significantly closer to success. This reality introduces an element of uncertainty – some projects might falter, while others flourish. Embracing this uncertainty is crucial; it fuels your potential. The best work of your life could be just around the corner. Without sticking to your goals and plans, you may never uncover what you're truly capable of. Isn't that a thought brimming with power? Even top achievers face regular failures, yet only a handful of significant successes can elevate them to brilliance. This principle applies to you too. Even if some of your ideas prove less than stellar, your unwavering self-discipline to persist holds immense value.

Even if what you produce initially seems lackluster, maintaining a positive perspective can pave the way for eventual triumph. A project's failure or a less-than-ideal outcome doesn't signify the end; it's a chance to learn. Instead of dwelling on failure, muster the courage to dissect why it fell short. Extract the lessons embedded within it. A failed project becomes a platform to refine your self-discipline. Spending hours daily on a project demonstrates your ability to focus and overcome procrastination, a valuable skill in itself.

Recognizing what works and building upon it is fundamental to sustained success. It might sound obvious – when something works, replicating it is wise, right? Yet, this process demands self-discipline. It requires stepping back and assessing what truly propels you towards your goals. Challenges arise when what you want to work and what actually works don't perfectly align. For instance, imagine you create video games. Although you and your fellow founder prefer classic arcade games, market research indicates a strong demand for car-themed racing games. Despite your personal preferences, you release a racing game, which receives significantly more positive reception and sales. Here, the self-discipline lies in setting aside personal biases and acknowledging the market's preference.

Taking an honest look at what works and what doesn't necessitates self-discipline and detachment from emotional investments. It's challenging because humans tend to continue investing in projects or ideas they've started, even when it's not beneficial. This attachment, known as the "sunk cost fallacy," can be detrimental. It's tough to admit a wrong decision when emotions are deeply invested. However, accepting that most efforts might not yield desired outcomes equips you with the wisdom to gracefully let go of unproductive ventures. It's not about celebrating failure; it's about recognizing the long-term benefits of sacrificing a fantasy to build on your current reality.

Ultimately, training yourself to focus on the present reality is far more productive than dwelling on "could bes" and "maybes." In the upcoming chapter, you'll delve into an Eastern therapeutic approach that teaches acceptance of reality while empowering steps for positive change.

19

Chapter 18: Morita Therapy

If you've ever experienced therapy, you're likely familiar with the Western counseling approach: identifying issues and working to conquer them through behavioral or cognitive adjustments. In this chapter, I'll introduce you to an alternative method for overcoming mental barriers and enhancing self-discipline: Morita therapy, a set of Japanese techniques that have empowered thousands to lead more peaceful, productive lives.

Morita therapy, founded by Japanese psychiatrist Shoma Morita a century ago, is rooted in the concept of "arugamama," which translates to "acceptance of the world as it is" in English. Morita emphasized that we need not change or process our emotions to lead fulfilled lives. Instead, acknowledging our feelings, accepting them, and then focusing on the steps toward our goals is key. Attempting to forcefully alter our emotions often backfires, trapping us in a cycle of negativity.

Morita proposed a two-part theory of human nature. The first desire is self-actualization, driving us to reach our full potential and pursue goals, forming the foundation of self-discipline. Simultaneously, we desire stability, often hesitating to pursue dreams that might lead to failure despite knowing the benefits of achieving them.

CHAPTER 18: MORITA THERAPY

Morita therapists emphasize the perils of excessive thinking. While reflection is necessary, excessive rumination worsens negative emotions. Morita therapy encourages redirecting focus from inner struggles to underlying desires. For instance, someone anxious in social situations focuses on the desire for better relationships rather than symptoms of panic, working on practical plans like outings or conversation practice.

Morita therapy challenges the Western approach to mental health, critiquing its reliance on labels over constructive living. Traditional Morita treatment involves four stages: complete rest to foster calmness, light activity to reconnect with the present, moderate physical work to shift focus externally, and engaging in practical tasks to divert attention from inner thoughts.

By understanding and implementing Morita therapy's principles, you can overcome mental barriers, enhance your self-discipline, and lead a more content and purposeful life.

Even though traditional Morita therapy typically occurs in a residential context, you can apply its principles to your life without going anywhere. The fundamental lesson is that action, not overthinking, is profoundly healing. While it might not eliminate all self-doubt and sadness, taking action helps you find meaning. It's normal not to always feel motivated to work towards your goals; your emotions in the moment don't define your success. The core of self-discipline lies in persisting even when you're tempted to give up. Don't be ashamed of your feelings; accept them and carry on. When you achieve your goal, what truly matters? Not your daily mood swings, but the fact that you persevered.

Self-talk is a valuable tool in implementing Morita principles. When you find yourself resisting work due to fear of failure or dwelling on past memories, talk to yourself out loud. Acknowledge your emotions and push yourself to keep going. While it might seem odd, this practice can make a significant difference. If speaking aloud isn't possible, use your inner voice or write motivating phrases on sticky notes.

Understanding the Morita framework reveals that you don't have to wait for confidence or be free from anxiety to take risks or face fears. Feelings fluctuate due to internal and external factors; they shouldn't be an excuse for inaction. Embrace Morita principles by tackling small tasks that make you uncomfortable or bored. For instance, cleaning your closet might seem tedious, but by accepting the boredom and doing it anyway, you'll find your internal resistance fading away. Practical work, approached mindfully, can be surprisingly calming.

Accepting your feelings might be unfamiliar in Western culture, which values problem-solving and logical reasoning. However, strong emotions often can't be reasoned away, especially during significant life events like breakups or loss. Morita therapy teaches that emotions, positive or negative, don't have to dictate your actions. Even when you're feeling low, you can still take constructive steps. By accepting your negative feelings and working alongside them, you can achieve meaningful results.

Morita therapy emphasizes the importance of proper rest. It's essential to take breaks from your busy life to prevent burnout. Working tirelessly isn't virtuous; in fact, it can lead to exhaustion. The next chapter will delve deeper into recognizing signs of burnout and strategies to prevent it from derailing your self-discipline.

20

Chapter 19: Preventing Burnout

In this chapter, we'll delve into a crucial aspect of self-discipline: recognizing and avoiding burnout. Despite your determination and resilience, pushing yourself excessively can have severe consequences. I'll guide you through understanding the signs of burnout, how to recover effectively, and why individuals can end up emotionally and physically drained due to overwhelming responsibilities. Remember, prevention is always better than cure.

First, it's essential to comprehend what burnout truly entails. Feeling stressed occasionally, especially during challenging work or personal periods, is normal. This stress might temporarily overwhelm you, causing a brief mental freeze. These moments of feeling overwhelmed are protective mechanisms, giving you a chance to regain control and reduce anxiety.

However, burnout is different. It represents a breaking point where someone can't cope mentally or physically with life's demands anymore. It manifests as exhaustion, low mood, hopelessness, and indecision. Burnout affects individuals irrespective of their roles – be it a high-powered executive or a full-time parent. Ironically, those with remarkable self-discipline are often more susceptible because they tend to take on too much and neglect self-care.

Preventing burnout involves harnessing your self-discipline differently.

Besides accomplishing tasks, you must learn to say "no" to projects that drain your energy and maintain a healthy routine. Prioritize sleep, hydration, and balanced meals, understanding that your decision-making ability diminishes when you're fatigued. Regular rest and nourishment ensure your willpower stays strong.

Moreover, dedicating time for relaxation and recreation is vital. Constant work without breaks leads to burnout. Even the most dedicated individuals, like Shaolin monks and Special Forces members, recognize the importance of downtime. When you relax, fully detach from work stress, applying principles from Morita therapy to give yourself a mental break.

Perspective is key to managing stress levels. In the grand scheme, your problems are often insignificant. While you strive for success, remember that failure isn't the end; it's a chance to learn and grow. Your mindset plays a crucial role. You can perceive work as a burden or as an opportunity for personal and professional growth. Applying positive thinking and self-discipline enables effective workload management and stress reduction. Avoiding procrastination and trivial distractions prevents tasks from piling up, reducing the risk of burnout.

Remember, even the most brilliant individuals need a structured approach. Don't fall into the trap of assuming everything will magically come together. Establishing a framework and managing your workload efficiently, coupled with self-discipline, will help you perform at your best without succumbing to burnout.

The most effective solution to the common problem of overwhelming tasks is proper scheduling. At the beginning of any project, take immediate action by outlining the necessary steps and estimating the time required realistically. If uncertain, seek advice from experienced individuals; assuming tasks might take one and a half times longer acts as a safeguard. This approach ensures you can use extra time if you finish early or not feel stressed if tasks take longer than planned.

Personally, I find this scheduling method invaluable, especially for tasks like report writing and presentations. Initially, when I started as a freelance consultant, I struggled to estimate the time needed, leading to stressful late nights or wasted gaps in my schedule. Over time, I learned the importance of maintaining a spreadsheet with task durations, aiding in planning my week effectively.

Often, people avoid planning due to fear – fear of acknowledging the hard work, challenges, and uncertainties ahead. However, confronting these feelings, acknowledging them, and still taking action is crucial. Confidence won't magically appear; it requires facing the task head-on, even if it means enduring some initial discomfort. Recognizing this early in your career promotes productivity and reduces stress.

While preventive measures are vital, if you're already experiencing burnout, it's crucial to prioritize rest. Just a week of mental and physical rest can restore balance. Be open with your employer, clients (if applicable), and doctor. Seeking help is your responsibility. Many employers are understanding about burnout, and discussing your situation with HR or your manager can lead to necessary support.

During recovery, reflect on the experience and learn from it. Burnout doesn't indicate failure but highlights the need for a change in your work approach. Cultivate self-discipline and learn from past mistakes. Analyze the signs that led to burnout and devise strategies to prevent a recurrence. Balancing pushing your limits and safeguarding your mental health is a skill that requires practice and adjustment.

21

Chapter 20: Embracing Change - Overcoming the Status Quo Bias

As you approach the end of this book, you've likely absorbed valuable lessons on enhancing self-discipline and applying it to your aspirations. Yet, you might encounter an invisible barrier hindering your progress. This common experience is rooted in a psychological phenomenon known as the "status quo bias," which can impede even the most determined individuals. In this chapter, we'll delve into this phenomenon, understanding how it operates, and empowering you to reclaim your self-discipline.

Psychologists have long studied self-defeating behaviors, among which the "sunk cost fallacy" and the lesser-known status quo bias feature prominently. This bias explains why people tend to cling to familiar situations, even when desiring change. It's the force that keeps us in expired relationships or mundane jobs despite opportunities for improvement.

In essence, the status quo bias denotes humanity's inclination to favor the familiar over the unknown, grounded in economic principles. Researchers Samuelson and Zeckhauser observed in 1988 that people often choose to maintain their current situation, even when presented with alternatives. Several factors contribute to this bias.

Firstly, loss aversion theory plays a role, as humans fear losing what they have, even if it isn't particularly fulfilling. Change demands effort and consideration, representing a tangible cost that many are unwilling to pay. Additionally, the fear of regret influences decisions. People dread making wrong choices, fearing judgment and believing that any change might backfire, leaving them worse off. This fear often paralyzes them into inaction, keeping them in their comfort zone.

The mere exposure effect, another psychological phenomenon, solidifies existing beliefs and routines. The more we encounter something, the more we accept and like it, even if it isn't ideal. This effect can both help maintain positive habits and hinder change efforts, making it difficult to break away from established routines.

Understanding the status quo bias enables self-reflection. Recall moments in your past when decisions or opportunities arose. Have phrases like "That's how I've always done it" or "If it ain't broke, don't fix it" influenced your choices? Recognizing these patterns is crucial. By fostering self-awareness and engaging your rational decision-making abilities, you can overcome the status quo bias. When faced with the choice between the familiar and the unknown, challenge yourself. Evaluate your options, and remember, change, though challenging, can lead to growth and fulfillment.

Create a four-part list to organize your thoughts logically and overcome the status quo bias. Divide a page into quarters and jot down: Advantages of the current situation, Disadvantages of the current situation, Advantages of the alternative under consideration, and Disadvantages of the alternative under consideration. Allocate at least ten minutes for this task. Review your lists after a good night's sleep. Seek input from a trusted friend or family member if needed, but remember to critically evaluate their advice due to the common tendency to succumb to the status quo bias.

Realize that your emotions shouldn't dictate your decisions. Negative feelings can coexist with action, and you can harness positive energy to propel yourself toward your goals. Embrace change anxiety as a normal part of growth. Understand that many worries stem from overthinking and pessimism, and taking action often reveals that fear is unwarranted. While small decisions like choosing lunch might not significantly impact your life, using these moments to practice rational decision-making can refine your approach. Challenge routine choices by actively exploring new options, from trying a different radio station to changing your eating habits or clothing style. Breaking these habitual patterns builds the confidence needed to tackle more substantial life changes like career shifts or ending unhealthy relationships.

Recognize that ingrained habits keep you in repetitive cycles. Attempting to change one aspect of your life in isolation rarely succeeds. Instead, cultivate a thoughtful, self-aware, and self-disciplined approach across various areas. Overcoming the status quo bias facilitates embracing change, making self-discipline and goal commitment more attainable. By avoiding the allure of the familiar and opening up to new possibilities, you empower yourself to pursue what truly fulfills you. The key lies in your actions; proactively chase your aspirations without fear, and embrace the excitement of the unknown future that awaits.

22

Chapter 21: The Dunning-Kruger Effect

As you enhance your self-discipline and conquer temptations, your confidence naturally grows. Acknowledging your achievements and occasionally rewarding yourself is essential. However, this chapter serves as a warning. Amidst your confidence, it's crucial to maintain realistic self-assessment. This chapter explores what happens when people lose their ability to accurately gauge their competence and how to prevent it.

Most people know someone who overestimates their skills, like a relative claiming a great sense of humor while telling terrible jokes. While you might have a more realistic view of your abilities, many tend to overestimate their competence in various areas. The Dunning-Kruger Effect describes a situation where someone not only lacks competence but is unaware of their limitations, creating a "double burden." Such individuals repeatedly make mistakes and struggle to correct them due to their lack of insight. They genuinely believe in their capabilities, attributing failures to bad luck.

Psychologists Justin Kruger and David Dunning found this effect in assessments of grammar, logic, and humor. Those objectively rated as the worst performers (bottom 25% of their group) exhibited the least accurate self-assessment. This lack of metacognitive abilities hampers their capacity to critically evaluate their understanding. For example, understanding grammar rules is essential not only for crafting sentences but also for evaluating the correctness of one's opinions.

Before this concept gained prominence, psychologists had noted people tend to consider themselves above average in various areas, including leadership and written expression. The Dunning-Kruger effect is an extreme version of this common human tendency. It has implications in different settings, explaining instances where seemingly incompetent individuals advance due to their lack of awareness, while genuinely competent people remain humble.

In the context of self-discipline, viewing it as a skill reveals the possibility of overestimating your ability. If you think you've mastered resisting temptation and staying productive constantly, be cautious. This research implies that expertise fosters humility, recognizing there's always more to learn. It's about balancing a positive self-image with openness to objective feedback. Avoid complacency and arrogance by remaining receptive to constructive criticism and acknowledging your deficiencies.

"Objective feedback" could be quantifiable goals like earnings or unbiased assessments by strangers. For instance, if you believe you're an excellent driver, taking an advanced driving test might provide objective feedback. A driving instructor's critique, indicating areas for improvement, serves as a valuable reality check.

Acknowledging our limitations can be challenging, but it's a necessary reality check we all require. This awareness prompts us to reflect on our direction and contemplate ways to enhance ourselves. To counter the Dunning-Kruger Effect, which leads to overestimating one's abilities, continuous self-improvement is key. Mastery in a skill enhances your ability to evaluate your competence accurately. Therefore, seize every opportunity to refine your skills.

Dunning and Kruger found that training individuals in problem-solving not only improved their skills but also provided insights into their performance relative to others. This principle applies beyond lab tasks to everyday skills and goal pursuits. In the realm of self-discipline, consistent application of techniques outlined in this book, like working despite lack of motivation or positive thinking, is crucial. Your self-awareness grows alongside your competence. The most disciplined individuals acknowledge occasional distractions and bad days but appreciate their progress while recognizing room for improvement.

Embrace a lifelong learning approach. Whether it's learning a martial art, advancing your career, or adopting a new hobby, never assume you've learned everything. Accessing information through the internet has never been easier. Enroll in online courses or use apps for daily knowledge or skill enhancement. Many are free and provide objective feedback, aiding in avoiding overconfidence while celebrating progress.

Additionally, protect yourself from the Dunning-Kruger Effect by engaging with those who have achieved what you aspire to achieve. Don't compare yourself unfavorably; instead, focus on the gap between your current and desired state. Interacting with leaders or role models often reveals their humility and continual pursuit of learning, emphasizing the importance of enduring failure for success.

Recognizing the Dunning-Kruger Effect in others might be tempting, but resist the urge. It's challenging to prove someone's suffering from it, and criticizing others' abilities can damage fragile egos. Don't assume immunity; understanding the psychology doesn't make you impervious. Embrace self-doubt as a sign of humility and a drive for improvement. Imperfections are part of life's beauty, allowing us space to grow. Stay mindful, positive, resilient, and remember, there's always room for progress. May your successes inspire you, each experience teach you, and may you continually set high standards for yourself.

Before you go, could I ask for your help? If you found value in this book, please share your experience on Amazon and leave an honest review. Your feedback means the world to me. If I've inspired you in any way, I'd love to hear about it! Additionally, if you had any issues with the book, please email me at contact@mindfulnessforsuccess.com. I'm constantly working to improve and provide more value to my readers.

Thank you, and best of luck! I believe in you and wish you all the best on your journey ahead!

www.ingramcontent.com/pod-product-compliance
Lightning Source LLC
LaVergne TN
LVHW020432080526
838202LV00055B/5153